BEGINNING COUNTRY FIDDLE

BEGINNING COUNTRY FIDDLE

by Marilyn Bos

Oak Publications
New York/London/Sydney

Cover design by Pearce Marchbank
Book design by Lamont Clifton Thomas
Photographs by David Allan
Drawings by Nancy Allan
Modelled by Todd Westphal
Typography and music engraving by MusiGraph Inc.

Copyright © 1984 by Oak Publications
A Division of Embassy Music Corporation, New York, NY.

Order No. OK 64725
International Standard Book Number: 0.8256.0294.7

Exclusive Distributors:
Music Sales Corporation
257 Park Avenue South, New York, NY 10010 USA
Music Sales Limited
8/9 Frith Street, London W1V 5TZ England
Music Sales Pty. Limited
120 Rothschild Street, Rosebery, Sydney, NSW 2018, Australia

Printed in the United States of America by
Vicks Lithograph and Printing Corporation

Dedicated to my Mother

Contents

The Left Hand Fingering

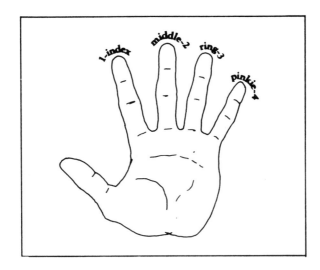

The Bow

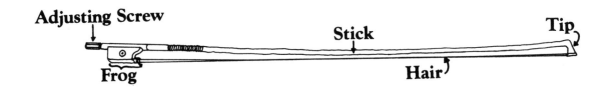

The Fiddle

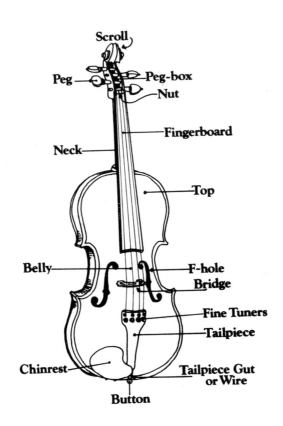

Lesson 1: Tuning

Figure 1

Figure 2

The pitches to which the fiddle is tuned are: E, A, D, G (Figure 1). The thinnest string is the high E pitch.

Use the pitch-pipe or a piano to accurately check your tuning.

Adjusters (Figure 2) are easy to tune when the instrument is slightly out of tune.

Use steel strings with the Adjusters.

The fiddle pegs are used when the instrument is out of tune. As you near the desired pitch, push the peg in so when you actually reach the pitch, the peg already has some traction.

Most fiddlers use a shoulder-pad. This is a soft pad of some sort like a dry sponge, or a shoulder-pad made particularly for the fiddle that lies between the instrument and the left shoulder.

Measure the distance from the front of your jaw to the top of your collarbone (Figure 3).

Figure 3

Now apply that measurement from the area of the chin-rest at its highest point to the underside of the fiddle (Figure 4).

Fill the extra space with a soft pad of some sort.

Figure 4

Exercise 1: Holding the Fiddle

Hold the fiddle like a guitar, scroll higher than the body of the instrument (Figure 5).

Figure 5

Slide the left hand back and forth along the fiddle. Repeat the movement about eight times. Create a smooth, fluid motion (Figure 6).

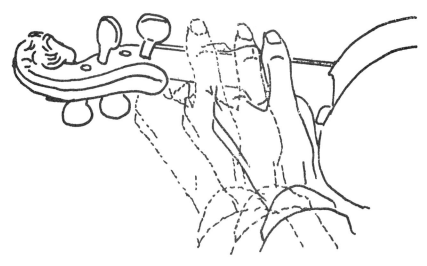

Figure 6

Exercise 2

Allow the left hand to lie passively against the rib of the fiddle.
Pluck the E and A strings at the same time with the little finger (Figures 7 & 8).
Now pluck the D and G with the little finger.

Figure 7
Plucking the E and A strings in Guitar position

Notice the space between the neck of the violin and the base of the thumb.

Figure 8
Plucking the E and A strings in guitar position viewed at a different angle.

Exercise 3:
Bringing the Fiddle Up In Position

Stand in front of a large mirror, left foot a bit forward (Figure 9).
Bring the fiddle straight forward in front of you (Figure 10).
Bring the instrument back closer to you.
Swing it up and place your first finger on the button of the fiddle (Figure 11).
With the first finger, now touch the indentation in the center of your throat (Figure 12).
Touch the button, touch the indentation.
Swing the fiddle up in position letting the button lie at the indentation of the throat (Figure 13).

Figure 9
Left foot a bit forward.

Figure 10
The fiddle - straight forward.

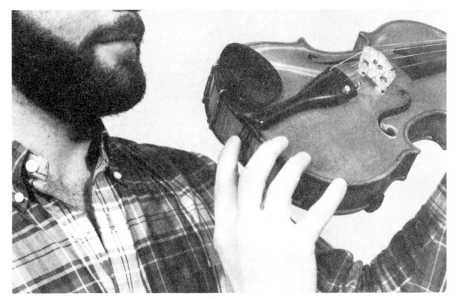

Figure 11
1st Finger on the button

Figure 12
Touch the indentation of the throat.

Figure 13
Violin up in position. Button lies comfortably at indentation of throat.

Exercise 4:

Take hold of the fiddle with your right hand (Figure 14).
Relax your head by moving it back and forth, up and down.
Support the fiddle with your right hand.

Figure 14

Slide your left hand back and forth along the neck as you previously did in guitar position (Figure 6.)
Now assume the plucking position you had in Exercise 2 (Figure 7). Pluck as you previously did, with the little finger (4th).
Pluck the highest pitched strings (E, A) eight times.
Pluck the lowest pitched (D, G) similarly.
The left hand is on the right side of the instrument (Figure 15).

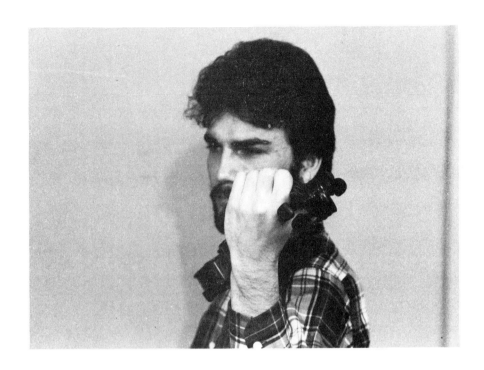

Figure 15
Left hand is on right side of the instrument.

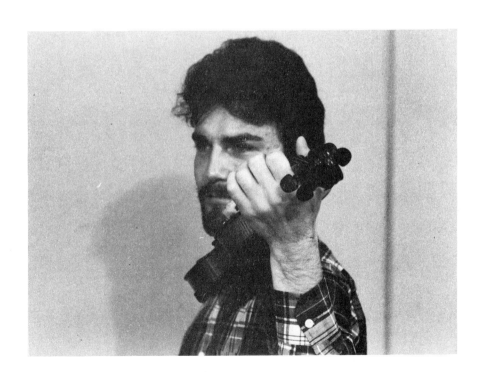

Figure 16
Not this! Where the left hand is partially under the neck of the fiddle.

Exercise 5: Plucking in circles.

After resting, with the fiddle down, repeat Exercise 3.

Figure 17

Now with the fiddle up in position, pluck with the 1st finger of your right hand.
Make large circles as you pluck. Develop a swing and a rhythm to your motion.
Keep the right arm moving in large circles – don't stop the motion.
Do the plucking at the end of the fingerboard nearest the bridge.
Pluck over the fingerboard, not in the open space right next to the bridge.
Pluck the E, A strings together eight times, then the D, and G.
This is a continual motion exercise. Don't stop your arm.
Plucking the strings with the finger is called *pizzicato*.
With the fiddle down, repeat Exercises 4 and 5 four more times, alternating them to
   familiarize yourself with the fiddle and to do motions which are common in
   actual playing.

Variation: Now stroll about the room as you do the exercises. This creates a feeling of
   ease in handling the instrument.

1. Pluck with Left Hand,
2. Pluck circle-wise with the Right Arm.

Exercise 6:
Holding the Bow

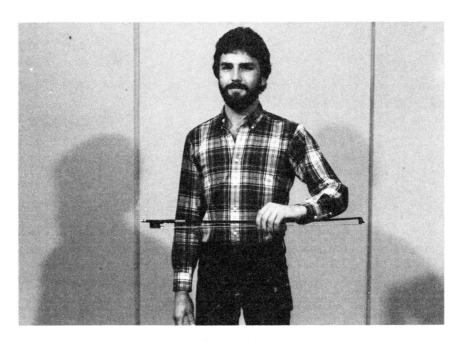

Figure 18
For now, hold the bow in the middle with the left hand.

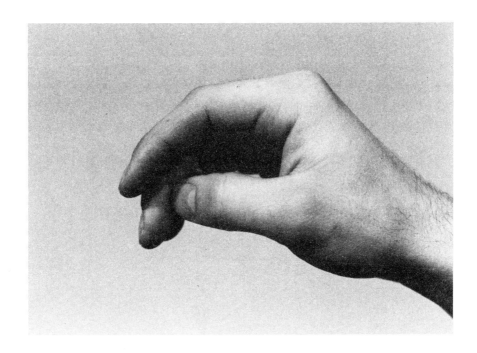

Figure 19
Make a circle with the thumb and 2nd finger of the right hand.

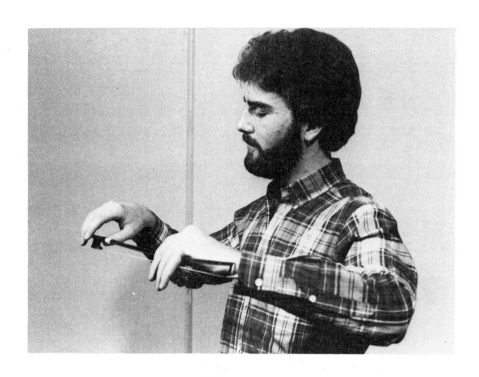

Figure 20
Slip the stick of the bow at the frog between the thumb and 2nd finger.

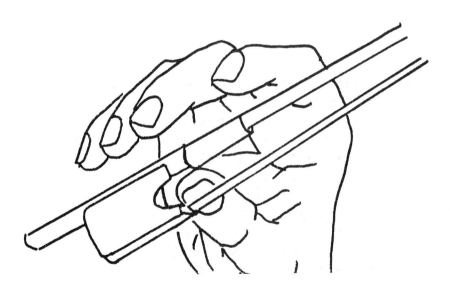

Figure 21
The thumb goes in the small space between the frog and the grip and points in an upward direction.

Figure 22

The Bow Hold: Notice the fingers are curved, including the little finger (it stands on top of the bow).

The thumb and 2nd finger are across from each other.

The 1st finger contacts the bow just below the middle joint, lying against the bone (Figure 22).

The 3rd finger is over the dot on the frog while the 4th finger is on top of the bow with more of it on your side than the other side.

All the fingers are curved, including the thumb.

The fingers are loose on the bow.

You don't need to hang on tightly – soon the bow will rest on the fiddle string and gravity will allow it to lie there.

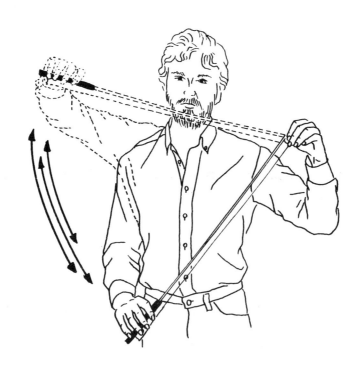

Figure 23
Raise and lower your arm.

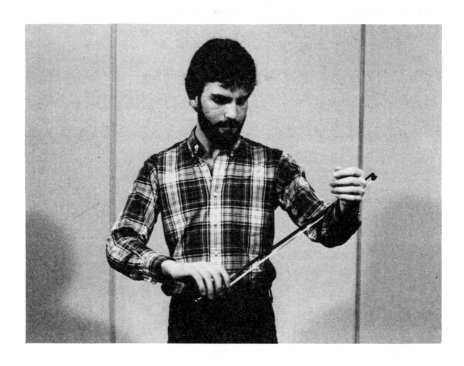

Figure 24

Repeat this Exercise (Figure 23):
This time, upon completion, transfer the bow to your left elbow joint from your left
  hand (Figure 24).
Move the bow up and down while letting it remain on your left elbow joint.

Repeat these rhythms 4 times while bowing on your left elbow joint:

Stop if you become tired!
It takes only a moment to relax.
Now begin again.

Lesson 2: Exercise 1 – Part 1

Now take up both violin and bow. Don't assume the bow hold yet, just hold the bow in
    a fist in your right hand (RH).
Repeat Exercise 3 (Lesson 1), to bring the fiddle up in position.
Once the fiddle is in position, hold it as you did before with the RH (Figure 14).
Move your head to loosen it and also the left shoulder.
Slide your left hand (LH) into plucking position (Figure 14).
Pluck the E-A strings several times with the LH, then the G-D to ensure that the LH
    is on the right side of the instrument (Figure 15).

Figure 25
Holding your bow on the strings against your left hand provides an excellent support
towards obtaining a firm bow-hold.

When you have gotten your rather loose bow-hold,
waggle your right arm to relax it and the shoulder.
Set the bow on the A string in the middle of the bow
midway between the bridge and the fingerboard.
Have the arm form an L-shape (Figure 26).

Figure 26

Exercise 1, Part 2.

Waggle your arm to loosen it. Let the weight of the bow fall in the string. Now move the bow back and forth at right angles to the string. Use about 5 inches of bow.

Keep the bow on an imaginary track midway between the bridge and the fingerboard.

Play 16 strokes on the A string and then 16 on the D string. Let the bow lie in the string. Don't clutch the bow. Take it easy. Gravity will support it on the string. Don't lift the bow off the string.

If you feel a little uncomfortable stop and get a new start. Don't try to play through tension. Tension can be relieved in a moment by giving yourself a breather and re-starting. Start from the beginning of the exercise!

Bowing Rhythms:

Leave the bow on the string during the rests.
⊓ = Down-Bow. When you see this marking move the bow from the area of the frog to the tip area.
V = Up-Bow. When you see this, move the bow from the tip area to the Frog area.

Play 3 times

Allow the weight of the bow to lie on the string.
The bow-hold has a clinging feeling – let the fingers be flexible.
The fingers have a curvature similar to their normal curve when you just allow your arm to hang at your side.
The shoulder is relaxed and passive; the arm feels lazy.

23

Exercise 2

Repeat Part 1 of the previous exercise to establish good fiddle position and a
   comfortable bow-hold.

Move the bow to the E string. Now move the bow at medium speed (no sound
   involved) back and forth across the strings (E to G) with an arced, semi-circular
   motion similar to that of the curvature of the bridge (Figure 27).

Figure 27
**Moving the bow medium speed across the strings. No sound involved. An arcing
motion, non-stop.**

Keep the arm moving smoothly with no angles or jerky motions.

The bow always lies in the string, never lifts off. Let gravity do the job!

Notice the infinite number of arm heights as you smoothly cross the strings.

The bow moves smoothly and fluidly across the strings. The arm moves
smoothly.

BOWING EXERCISES. String crossings are a mainstay of country fiddling.

These are basic string crossing patterns:

Now play this exercise backwards

24

Lesson Three: String Crossings.

Middle of the bow.
Keep on the track. (Stay midway between the bridge and fingerboard.)
Use the same amount of bow for each bow-stroke.
Use a medium bow-speed.

Divide your bow accurately.

Now play this pattern backwards.

I love my fid-dle, I love my fid-dle

No Holds Barred

Advanced

Two or more notes sounded simultaneously are called *double-stops*. Play the double-stop accompaniment to this tune.

Red River Valley

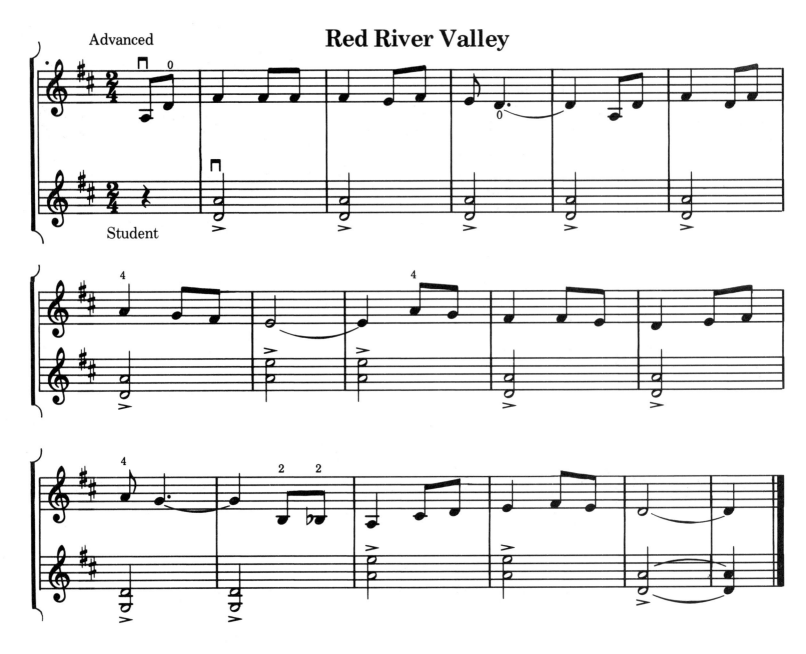

> = accent. Move the bow rapidly at the beginning of each double-stop, then slow it down suddenly. The difference in the sudden fast to the sudden slow bow speed will make the accent.

Review the basic bowings on page 23.
Add these bowings:

Practice on all strings.

Lesson Four: More String Crossings

Leave the bow on the string. Move smoothly from one string to the next.

You can put a little more weight on the bow when you play double-stops.

Most of the time the first note of a measure will be down-bow.
This is because it is easier to make a heavier sound on the down-bow.

Exercise 1

Hold the fiddle like a guitar.
Slide the left hand back and forth along the neck as in Figure 6.
Upon completion, let the hand come smoothly to rest at the end of the finger-board nearest the pegs (Figure 6.)
Place the tip of the 1st finger on the A string –the pitch B.

Pluck the 1st finger pitch several times with the right thumb.

Check your hand position (Figure 28).

Figure 28
Left hand position – 1st Finger Placement

Your hand position will probably be quite good following the easy movement back and forth along the fingerboard.

Notice that there is a space between the neck and the base of your thumb (Figure 6).

Figure 29
The left hand is on the right side of the instrument whether in guitar position or up in playing position

Notice that you are face to face with your 1st fingernail when you are on the A string.
The joint of the 1st finger is slanted slightly toward the scroll.

Note the position of the "palm" joint of the 1st finger while fingering on the A string as seen in Figures 30 and 31.

The 3rd joint of the 1st finger (the joint nearest the palm of the hand) can rest anywhere from very slightly above the fingerboard to a little below the fingerboard depending upon the length of your fingers (Figures 30 and 31).

Figure 30
For average length fingers, the height of the "palm" joint will probably be about the same as the fingerboard

Figure 31
For shorter fingers, the height of the "palm" joint will be a little below the fingerboard.

When fingering on the G string, the "palm" joint will be higher; on the E string it will be a little lower.

Exercise 2

Each time you play these exercises, precede them by sliding the hand back and forth along the neck several times to establish a relaxed, comfortable feeling.

Guitar position – Scroll higher than body of instrument. Pluck with thumb of right hand.

0 = Open string.

Practice these open string bowings:

Exercise 3

Practice the "Bringing the fiddle Up in Position" exercise (Exercise 3, page 12).

Support the fiddle with your right hand and move your head off the chin-rest to release any tension (Figure 14).

Move your left hand back and forth along the neck, come to rest in position as before and pluck the 1st finger B.

Check your hand position.

Pluck A and B above. After you have practiced them, start playing them with the bow.

Arco is the Italian term meaning "with the bow."

Lesson Five:

"The Gopher Gambol"

Play this in the following ways:
1. Guitar position – *Pizzicato* (pluck)
2. In playing position – *Pizzicato* (Figure 32).
Place the right thumb on the edge of the fingerboard.
Pluck with the 1st finger over the fingerboard a little.
3. *Arco* (with bow)

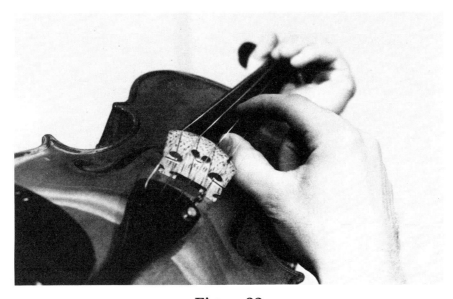

Figure 32

The Gopher Gambol

Marilyn Bos

31

The Elbow Float (Bow Strokes with Releases)
    (Preparation) for "Dance Floor Waltz")
    Start the bow stroke in the middle of the bow.
    Swing your elbow up a little as you start each note.
    Then allow gravity to take its course and your arm will fall into the correct
    position as you begin to play the next note.

    This is a non-stop action. Keep your arm moving.
    Stay on the string throughout. Don't lift the bow off the string.
    Notice this technique in the last two bars of "Dance Floor Waltz."

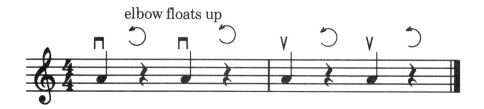

elbow floats up

Figure 33
Down bows

Figure 34
Up bows

Dance Floor Waltz

Rhythms and string crossings on open strings

Principles of Tone Production

Listen to your sound as you play these exercises.

Is it a good sound – strong, with clarity and beauty?

Or is it scratchy? Does it sound thin? After all, the reason why we play the fiddle is because we like the way it sounds!

And the sound is produced chiefly by the bow arm.

The three factors in tone production that, working together, produce a cultivated, refined sound.

1. The point of contact of the bow on the string.

Keep the bow parallel to the bridge, and at a right angle to the string.

Bow midway between the bridge and the fingerboard.

2. The speed of the bow.

This has to do with how fast you are moving or "drawing" the bow on the string.

Right now we are drawing medium speed strokes in the middle of the bow.

3. The weight of the bow on the string.

We are letting the bow sink into the string under the natural weight of the arm.

Let's put a little weight into the bow through the 1st finger and press the end of the 2nd finger slightly into the frog.

A General Rule:

When playing on the E string, you usually can use more bow or less weight, and can play closer to the bridge.

When playing on the G string, you can use less bow or more weight and not play as close to the bridge.

In other words: the thicker the string, the more relaxed weight you can roll into the bow, but you cannot play as close to the bridge or use as much bow as you can with a thinner string.

Experiment with this on the previous bowings (Figures 33, 34).

Lesson 6: The Left Hand – Adding the 2nd finger (0 - 1 - 2)

Exercise 1: This is similar to Exercise 1 in Lesson Four.

Hold the fiddle like a guitar.
Slide the left hand back and forth along the neck.
Come to rest at the end of the fingerboard nearest the pegs.
Place the tip of the 1st finger on the note B.
The 1st fingernail will point toward your face.
Place the 2nd finger the same distance from the 1st finger as the 1st finger is from the nut.

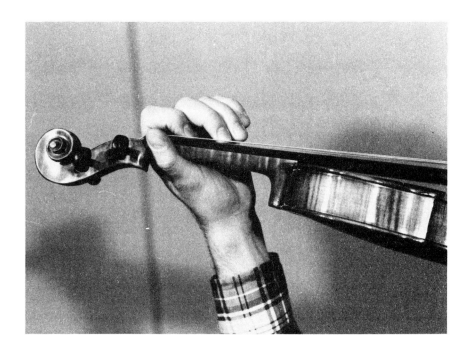

Figure 35

Whereas the 1st fingernail points toward you, the 2nd fingernail will be more at an angle (Figure 35).

The 2nd finger will be right next to the 3rd.

Exercise 2

Pluck 0 - 1st - 2nd fingers back and forth four times each, in rhythm.
    Practice the following in three ways:
    1. In guitar position
    2. Pluck in playing position
    3. After a few days, play *arco*

Keep the 1st finger on the string when playing with the 2nd finger.

Figure 36

The left arm will be a little further underneath the instrument when playing on the G string.
The bow arm will be higher.

Figure 37

The left arm will not be as far underneath the instrument when you are playing on the E string.
The bow arm will be lower than on the other strings.

Exercise 3

1. Pluck in guitar position
2. Pluck in playing position
3. After a few days, play *arco*

Keep the 1st finger on the strings throughout in the accompaniment, if possible. The line after "1" indicates this.

Lesson 7:

Exercise 1 Some Basic Arpeggios

An arpeggio is a broken chord.

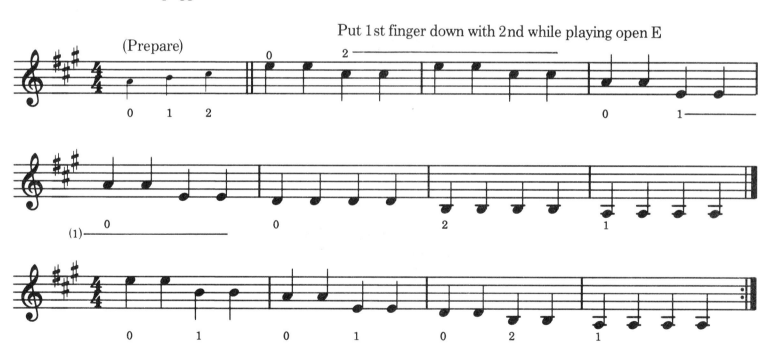

Check your bow hold (Figure 21).
Are your fingers curved somewhat?
Is your little finger on top of the bow?
Is your thumb curved, pointing upward?
Is your thumb in the small space between the frog and the grip (Figure 20).

Exercise 2 The Crawl Stroke

1. Set the middle of the bow on the A string.
2. Waggle your arm like a Raggedy Ann doll to relax the arm and shoulder.
3. Arc the bow soundlessly across the strings from E to G and back to create a feeling of ease in the arm (Figure 27).
4. Swing back to the A string and start moving the bow in short strokes (not more than 5) from the middle to the tip.

After reaching the tip move back with these short strokes until you are at the frog.

"Crawl" back and forth in this manner several times to feel what it's like to play in all areas of the bow.

Keep your arm moving when you are at the frog so you won't have to start the motion again at the beginning of the new ⊓ stroke.

Some good advice:

When you move toward the tip, the ⊓ will be the longer stroke; back toward the frog, the ⋁ will be longer.

Take your time.

Keep the bow midway between the bridge and the fingerboard.

Practice "Ida Red". in the usual three ways:

1. In guitar position
2. Pluck in playing position
3. *arco*

Look at the fiddler in Figure 38.

Notice that he leans his head slightly to the left.

Your head should be slightly toward the left or vertical. Never lean your head to the right.

The head should support the fiddle side, not the bow side.

Figure 38

Exercise 3
Review "Sliding Along the Neck" (Figure 14).

Practice this exercise daily including the left hand plucking which ensures a good left hand position.

Exercise 4
Here are some key country fiddle rhythms for review.
Play each measure several times on each open string.

When you practice your open string bowings, your left hand should lie comfortably against the rib of the fiddle (Figure 14).

Use the middle of the bow. Keep the bow on the string during the rest.

"Pierrot's Place"

1. In guitar position (pluck)
2. In playing position (*pizz.*)
3. *arco*

Stay on the string throughout.
Make your release motion where indicated by arrow.

Pierrot's Place

Lesson 8: Exercise 1 Lifting the Bow off the String.

1. Set the middle of the bow on the A string.
2. Lift the bow about 4″ straight up off the string.
3. Set it back on the string soundlessly.
   Let the arm relax the bow into the string.
   Let the weight of the bow sink in the string.

Exercise 2 Practicing Down Bow (⊓) Circle Strokes.

1. Use the middle of the bow. Draw a short (about 5″) ⊓ stroke.
2. When you lift the bow off the string, make a small circle in the air before setting down for the next note.
3. Set the bow down soundlessly as before and rest in the string for a moment.

Bow Strokes for "Crawdad."

Example 1. Swing your arm higher to go form the D to the G string. Do it smoothly. (Figure 39.)

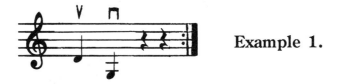

Example 1.

Example 2. Swing your arm down to go from the D to the A string. (Figure 40.)

Example 2.

Stay on the string for these exercises.

Figure 39
Starting Up Bow

Swing your arm higher to go from a higher pitch string to a lower pitch string (like D to G).

Figure 40
Starting Down Bow

Swing your arm lower to go from a lower pitch string to a higher pitch string. (like D to A). Keep the bow parallel to the bridge.

41

"Crawdad"

1. In guitar position (pluck)
2. In playing position (*pizz.*)
3. *arco*

Notice where to lift off the string.

Crawdad

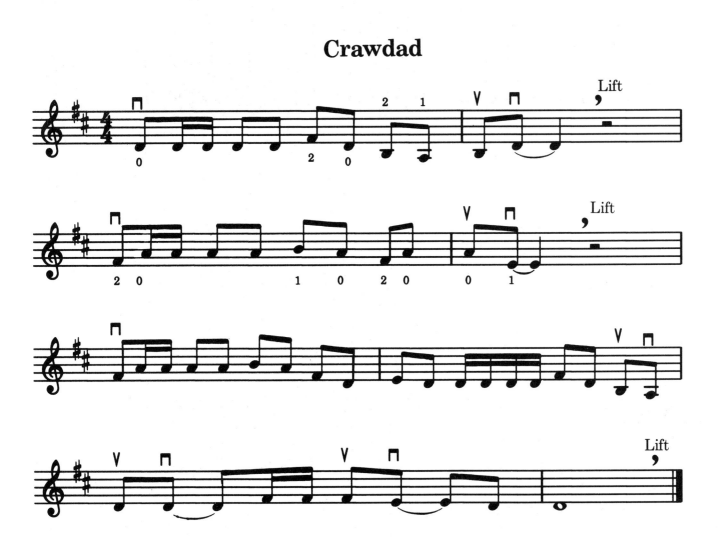

Lesson 9:

The Left Hand – Adding the 3rd Finger (0 - 1 - 2 - 3

  Λ is the symbol for one finger to be placed very close to the next.

  Learn it well. This symbol appears only in instructional books.

Exercise 1

  Hold the fiddle like a guitar.

  Slide the left hand back and forth along the neck.

  Upon completion of the eighth time let the hand come smoothly to rest at the end of the fingerboard nearest the pegs.

  Place the 1st finger on the note B on the A string, then the 2nd finger on the C♯.

  Pluck each pitch rhythmically four times before moving to the next pitch.

  The 2nd and 3rd fingers are very close to each other in a half step interval.

  The fingers slant toward the scroll.

  1. Pluck in guitar position

  2. Pluck in playing position (*pizz.*) in Figure 9.

  3. *arco*

  Practice these exercises three times, rest, then practice three times more.

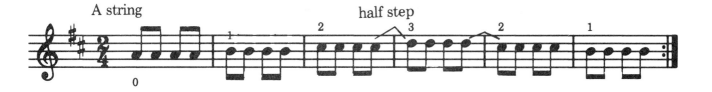

As you add fingers, keep the previous ones on the string.

43

This is the same finger pattern on the E string.
Listen to your sound.
On the E string, play closer to the bridge and use a little more bow with the same weight you used on the A string.

E string

G string

String Crossings
These string crossings are good practice for "Bile Them Cabbage Down."
Swing your elbow up while crossing from the A to the D string.

(Prepare)   Place 1st finger also

(Prepare)   Place 1st finger also

In this next version of "Bile Them Cabbage Down," "drive" the eighth note.
This means play it energetically – impel the arm forward on the eighth note.

Make the sixteenth notes afterthoughts, played more with the bow hand than
the bow arm.
If you hold the bow loosely, the fingers will automatically move in reaction to the
bow change.

In other words, the first note of every three is the more important.

Bile Them Cabbage Down

Play slowly at first.

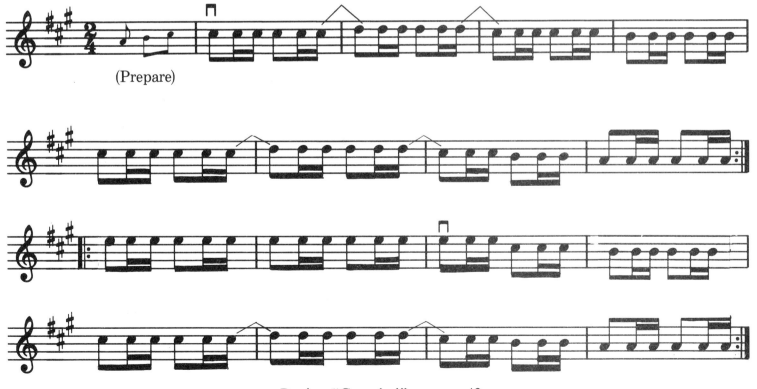

Review "Crawdad" on page 42.

Lesson 10: Independence of the Fingers (Left Hand)

The fingers of the left hand operate from the knuckle joint.

Figure 41

Correct   Wrong

Do not squeeze your fingers against each other as that will inhibit their action from the knuckle joint.
Each finger operates independently of the others and of the hand.
The fingers may touch each other in playing, however.

The most widely used keys for country fiddle music are D major, A major and G major.

Listen to your octave pitch.

46

Put your 2nd finger down with the 3rd finger.

Keep your fingers down where possible in the next three tunes.

Sweet Betsy From Pike

Salty Dog

Old Blue

Lesson 11: Double Stops

1. Arm higher and more weight on the bow for D and G double-stop;

   Follow the arc of the bridge in the string crossing motion.

2. Arm lower and use more bow for A and E double-stop:

   Follow the arc of the bridge.

3. In this faster string crossing, the arm precedes the bow.
   Swing the arm down first and the bow will follow.

4. In this yet faster string crossing, the arm will remain at the double-stop level and the crossing will be made with the wrist.

   To practice this string crossing, while doing the down-bow, keep the bow-stick directly above the bow hair.
   On the up-bow slant the stick toward the scroll.
   The crossing is thus being made in the wrist (Figures 42 and 43).

Middle of the bow

Slow crossing: follow the arc of the bridge.
The arm and the bow cross at the same time.
Medium speed crossing: precede the bow with the arm.
Fast crossing: use the wrist.

Figure 42
Bow stick high on down-bow. Fast string crossing.

Figure 43
Bow stick slanted on up-bow. Fast string crossing.

No Holds Barred

Double-stops: Support the string with your arm height.

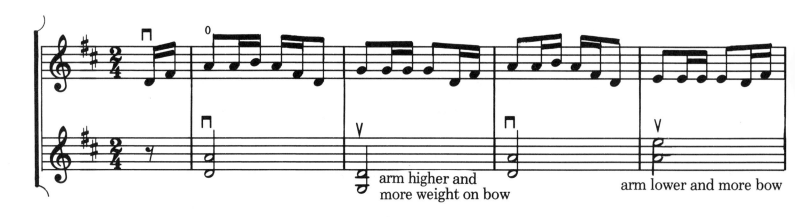

arm higher and
more weight on bow

arm lower and more bow

arm higher

arm lower

Continue playing "No Holds Barred", gradually increasing speed.

Holding the Fiddle at the Jaw

First, rest the fiddle against your chest.
Put leverage on the lip (the highest part) of the chin-rest (Figure 44).
Do this by pressing against the lip with your hand in such a way as to cause the scroll to rise.

Figure 44
Pressing against the lip of the chin rest causes the scroll to rise.

Substitute the jaw for the fingers.
    The weight of the jaw falls on the back part of the chin rest.
    Leverage correctly applied will cause the scroll to rise as before (Figure 45).

Figure 45
Weight of the jaw rests on back part of chin rest.

Don't let the weight of the chin come down in the center of the chin rest.
This will push the fiddle down.
The scroll should be at least level with the body of the fiddle and perhaps a little higher.

Good posture plays an important role in playing the fiddle.
Like a fine athlete, the fiddler whose moves are made efficiently and with an economy of effort produces the best performance.
Only the necessary energy is used.
No grinding hard work and strain are involved.

The "I Surrender Dear" Move.
Stand as shown in Figure 46, left arm extended.

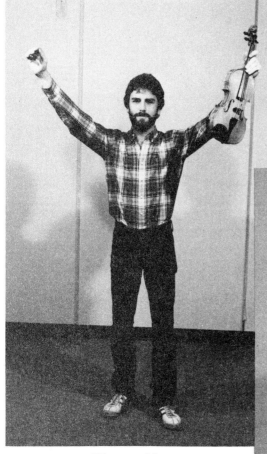

Figure 46
"I Surrender Dear"

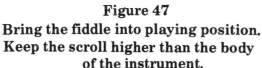

Figure 47
Bring the fiddle into playing position.
Keep the scroll higher than the body
of the instrument.

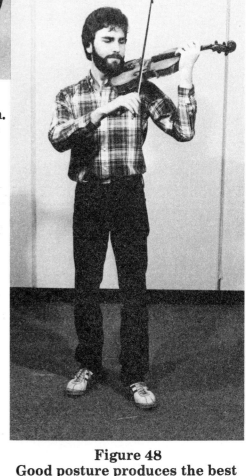

With the fiddle in position, locate the weight of the jaw on the back part of the chin rest as before.
Hold this position for a few seconds.
Do this exercise once every other day.

Most of the time you will support the fiddle by letting it lie on a "shelf" which is your collarbone and holding it with the left arm and hand.
Sometimes, however, you must support the fiddle at the jaw and shoulder, for instance when you slide your left hand back and forth along the neck in performance.

Figure 48
Good posture produces the best
results and saves energy!

Slurs. The marking ⌒ over or under ‿ notes means that those notes are to be played in the same bow stroke.

In this next exercise, the first two notes are both in the down-bow stroke, the next two are both in the up-bow.
These are slow string crossings, so follow the arc of the bridge to make the crossing smooth.

On the Ranch

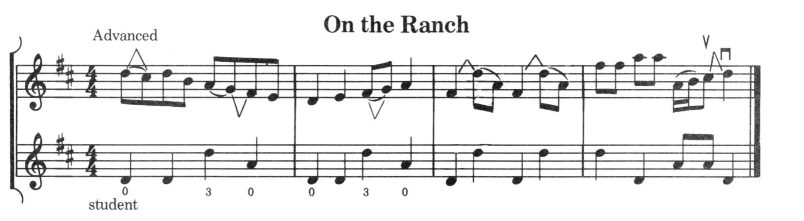

Arkansas Traveler

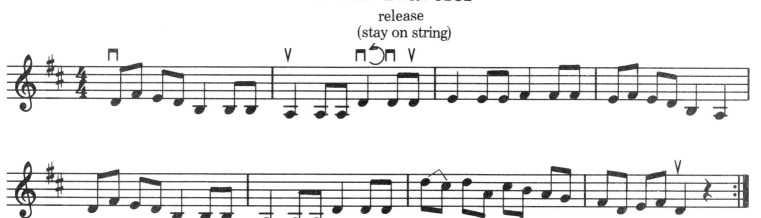

Lesson 12:

Continue your slur practice.
    Follow the contour of the bridge.
    Stay as close as you can to the next string prior to the actual crossing.
    Be aware of the bow!

Preparation for "Sourwood Mountain"

Sourwood Mountain

Left hand exercise
    Practice *pizzicato* and *arco*

Place 2nd finger with 3rd.

Figure 49

Down bow   **Up bow**

Using the upper half of the bow
    Play this A major scale using the upper half of the bow, that is, the area from the middle to the tip.
    Keep the bow parallel to the bridge as always.
    At the end of the down-bow the arm moves a little forward.
    Initiate this motion at the elbow.
    Do not raise the arm in accomplishing this forward motion.
    The arm moves back a little (initiated at the elbow) at the start of the up-bow.
    These motions enable the bow to keep a straight track on the string, parallel with the bridge.

A Major Scale

This finger pattern is the same as you have played so far, 0 - 1 - 2 - 3. One half step between 2nd and 3rd fingers.

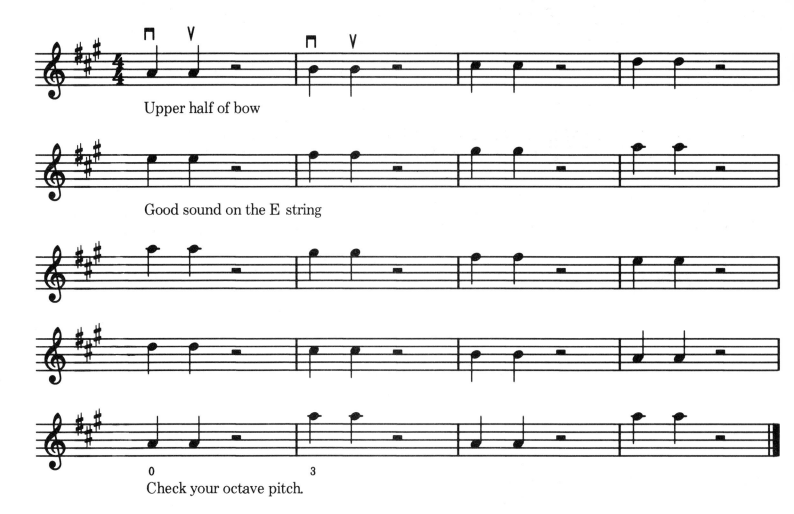

Upper half of bow

Good sound on the E string

Check your octave pitch.

Use the hand – either the fingers (preferably) – or the wrist to move the bow.
Don't use the arm.
Make the bow hold loose and relaxed, so the fingers will be supple.
The fingers will react to the bow changes; you'll see them move a little.
Ordinarily they will be more curved on the down-bow than the up-bow.

G Major Scale
Middle of the bow. Use tiny bow strokes — about an inch long. Play fairly rapidly.
Keep the bow-arm relaxed.

More Double-stops
Double-stops enhance many fiddle tunes.
Here is some double-stop practice which will aid you in harmonizing tunes in D
major.

1. *Pizzicato*   2. *Arco*

Upper half of the bow

Pluck with circular motion

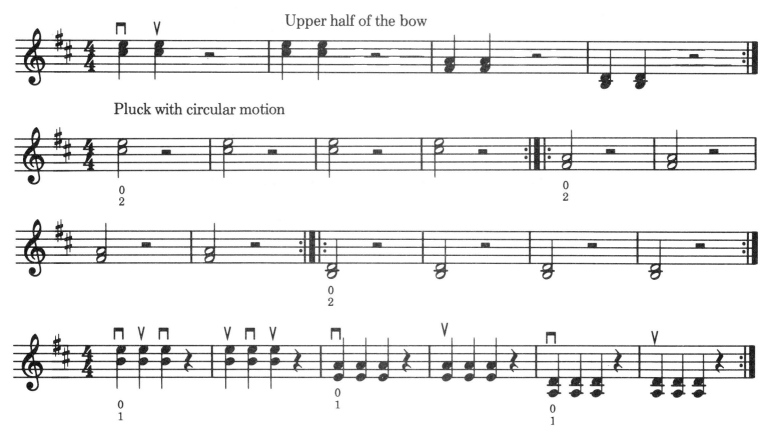

Go back to "No Holds Barred" (page 50) and "Arkansas Traveler" (page 53) and
play them a little faster.

Lesson 13: Basic Chords in D major

In the key of D major there are three basic chords with which to harmonize a tune:

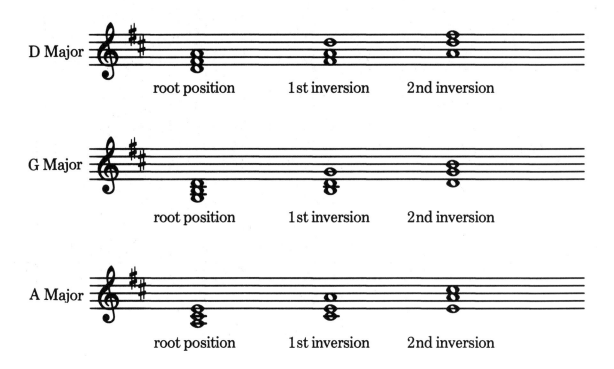

Here is a chart showing all the notes in first position.

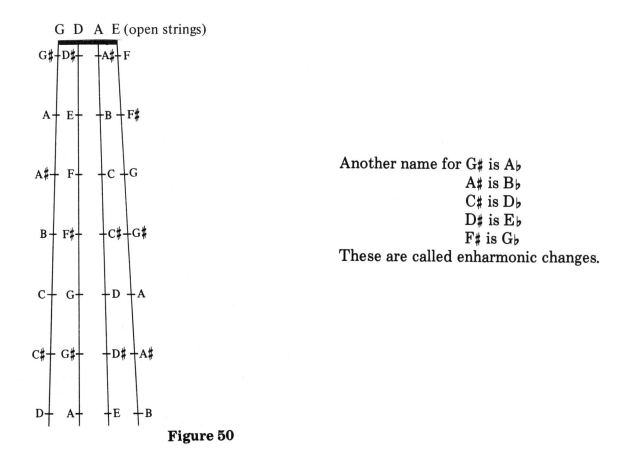

Another name for G♯ is A♭
A♯ is B♭
C♯ is D♭
D♯ is E♭
F♯ is G♭
These are called enharmonic changes.

Figure 50

Chords: D   G   D   A

Pluck in a
circular motion

Variation
pizz.

G   D   A   D

More Slur Practice
   Smooth string crossings! The sound is connected; no gaps.
   The arm moves in a rounded fashion, following the contour of the bridge.

Figure 51
Slurred String Crossing.

Keep arm and bow moving.

Reverse the bowing.

Rounded motion in the bow arm.

60

In the accompaniment to "The Eighth of January" check the pitch of your octaves with the open string.

Place your 2nd finger with your 3rd.

Rounded motion on the string crossings.

The Eighth of January

Lesson 14: Varying the Bow Speed

Use the same amount of bow for all the notes, no matter how long or short their duration. Vary the speed of the stroke to accomplish this.

Remember! The 2nd finger goes down with the 3rd finger.

Cumberland Gap

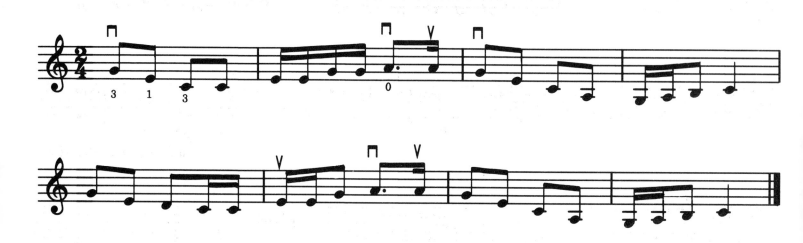

Preparation for "Old Dan Tucker"
Fast string crossing:

Move fast on 1st stroke

Slow string crossing:

Take your time on 1st stroke

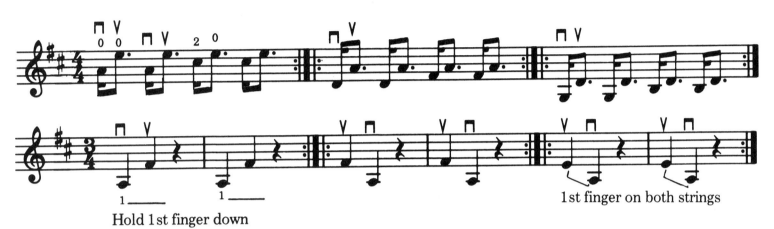

Hold 1st finger down

1st finger on both strings

Arm height high when on G string.
Swing arm into new string height.

Old Dan Tucker

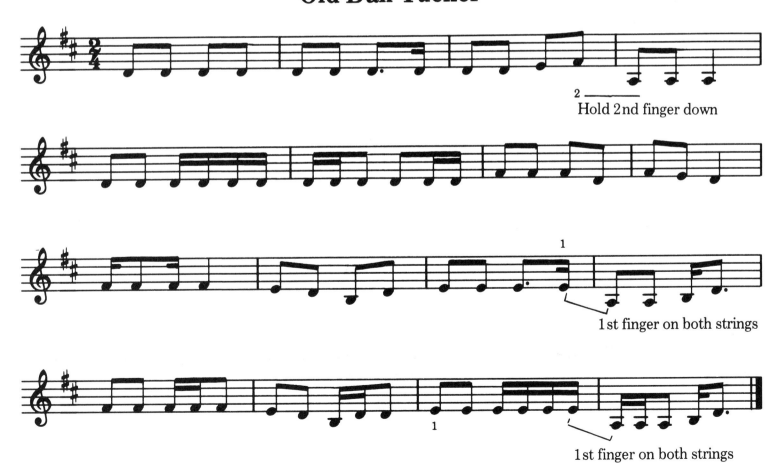

Hold 2nd finger down

1st finger on both strings

1st finger on both strings

Lesson 15: Bow Lifts

Review Exercises 1 and 2, Lesson 8.

Practicing down-bow circle strokes.

Whereas this motion was in the middle of the bow, now do it about 6″ from the frog.

1. Set the bow on the A string about 6 inches from the frog. Draw a short down-bow stroke.

2. Lift off the string with a small circular motion.

3. Set the bow down soundlessly and rest in the string for a moment. Repeat several times.

Practicing down-bow circle strokes at the frog.

Use the same motion as in the last exercise, but this time set down right at the frog.

Keep your arm moving throughout.

Don't stop the arm at the beginning of the down-bow.

Keep it moving at the same (medium) speed.

Particularly concentrate on moving through the stroke as you get in the frog area where the bow may seem bulky and heavy. Keeping the arm moving at constant speed through this area alleviates any awkward feeling you might otherwise have.

Frog-Use 1/2 bow

Repeat four times on each string.

For the release, lift off the string in a circular motion.

Release in this manner on the down-bow at the end of a phrase or the end of a composition.

The Bounce Bow (*Spiccato*)

Sometimes in country fiddle playing we bounce the bow on the string, letting it leave the string for variety or clarity in our playing.

Here is the initial practice for this technique:

1. Slide the entire bow hold about 3″ toward the tip of the bow. Keep the fingers and thumb in their usual relationship (Figure 53).

2. Bounce the bow experimentally on the A string using your usual down- and up-bow motion.

Allow the bow to leave the string at the end of each stroke.

Stay close to the string and keep your arm moving through the stroke (Figure 51).

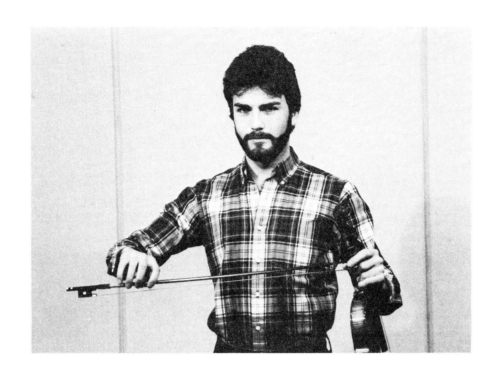

Figure 52
The bounce bow hold.

Figure 53
Bouncing the bow.

Bounce the bow: Practice these rhythms eight times each.

In this next bounce bow exercise, let the up-bow be the rebound to the down-bow stroke.
In other words, produce the down-bow through your arm motion, and the up-bow will return to you on its own.

Rebound

You will feel more weight on the 3rd and 4th fingers than when you stay on the string.
The weight won't be on the 1st finger at all. Keep the fingers curved, particularly the 3rd and 4th.
Let the weight fall on the back part of your hand (3rd and 4th fingers.)

Keep your arm moving through the strokes and through the rests.

Basic Chords in A major
In the key of A major there are three basic chords with which to harmonize a tune:

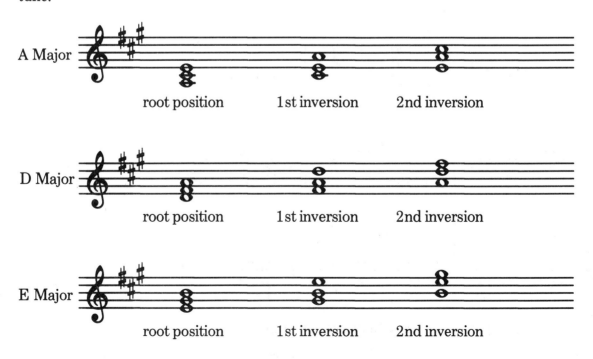

A Major — root position — 1st inversion — 2nd inversion

D Major — root position — 1st inversion — 2nd inversion

E Major — root position — 1st inversion — 2nd inversion

Practice the accompaniment to "Billy Boy" on the string at first with a strong sound.

Then bounce the bow with your high bow hold (bounce bow hold). When you play the melody, play the open E string for now, not the 4th finger.

Bow Division

In the following excerpt, move into the upper half of the bow so you will have enough bow for the long note B.

This takes some forethought and is an example of good bow division.

Billy Boy

Lift off string on last note with circular motion.

Lift off string on last double-stop with circular motion. Let the pitches ring.

Review previous pieces: "On The Ranch," "Cumberland Gap," "Eighth Of January," and "Old Dan Tucker" for ease of performance.

Lesson 16: The Left Hand – Adding the 4th Finger (0 - 1 - 2 ⌃3 ⌃4)

Place the 4th finger very close to the 3rd finger as shown in Figure 54.

This is not the usual position for the 4th finger in this particular 1-2-3 finger pattern, but it is a comfortable position to begin with.

Keep the little finger curved if possible.

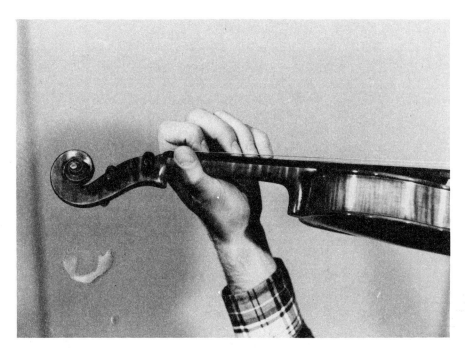

Figure 54

Practice the next pattern daily with the idea of curving and strengthening the little finger.
When you play your pieces, forget about the curvature and have fun playing.

In playing position: *Pizzicato*, then *Arco*.
Pause slightly before you start to play on the next string.

(Prepare)

In this next piece play the notes with dots (♩) short.
Short notes played on the string are called *staccato*. Play the notes with lines (♩) long. These are called *tenuto* or *sostenuto*. Develop contrast and variety in your playing.

Lazy Days

Stay on string

This next composition is a difficult piece to hear.
Have someone play along with you on the piano, if possible.
You can aid your intonation (pitch) by checking your 3rd finger. D on the A string
with the open D string.
Place your 2nd finger F♯ right next to the D.
Be sure the F♯ is in tune.

Lift off the string with your circle stroke where indicated. Keep your fingers
down (left hand).

Lifts and Flats

Lesson 17: The Left Hand (0 - 1 - 2̑ - 3 - 4)

Here is the usual position for the 4th finger in this finger pattern. The 3rd and 4th fingers are a whole step apart.

If you have trouble reaching the 4th finger E at first, slide into it lightly from the E♭ position.

This will relax your hand. Release the finger weight until you have reached the E.

The finger should be on the string during the slide.

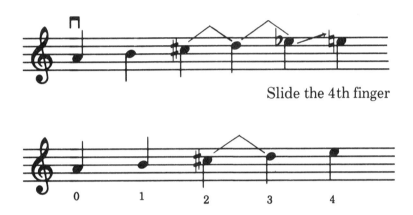

Slide the 4th finger

Figure 55

71

Practice *pizzicato*, then *Arco*.
Hit on the finger tip.
Curve your fingers.
Keep your fingers down.

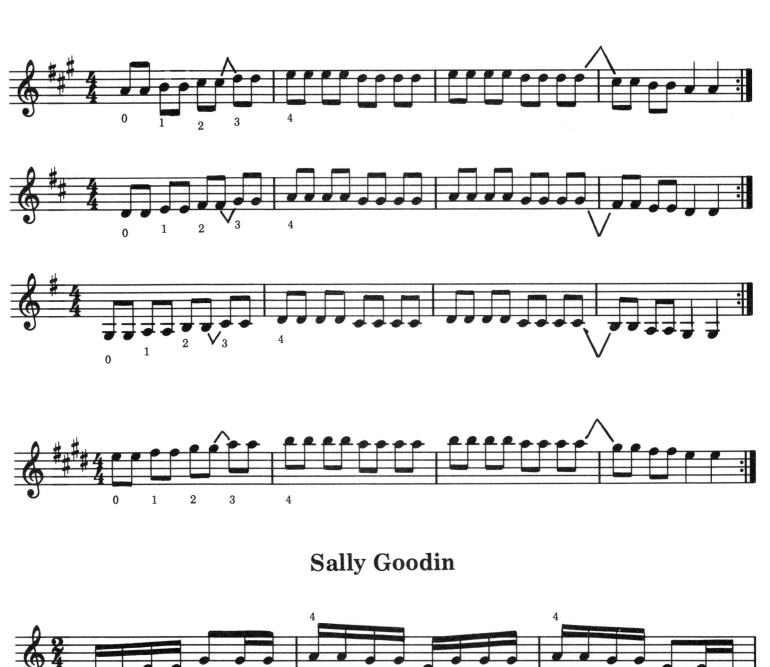

Sally Goodin

Review
D major scale and arpeggios.
Slant your fingers toward the scroll.
Keep your fingers down.

Turn back and play "Billy Boy" using the 4th finger instead of the open E string.

Lesson 18:

When you place the 4th finger, put the 3rd finger down also, in position to play.

Slurs

Review the slurs Lesson 11.

4. D major scale and arpeggio with close up slurs in the upper half of the bow.

Put 3rd finger
down with 4th.

3rd and 4th together

Shuffle Bowing

The shuffle bow pattern is a basic country fiddle (bluegrass) repeated rhythm.

At its most basic it is: ♩ ♫ ♩ ♫

This next scale uses shuffle bowing.

Cripple Creek
(Shuffle Bowing)

Var. 1

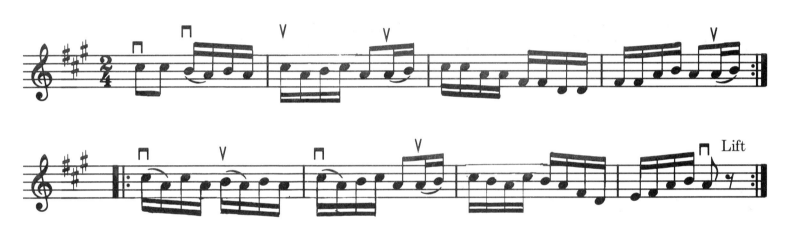

Var. 2

Lesson 19: More String Crossings

Fast string crossings.
>   Have the arm at double-stop height and cross with the wrist. Review number 4,
>   Lesson 11, for information on the stick slant.
>   Your shoulder should be passive.
>   There is some lower arm (elbow to wrist) movement, but concentrate on the
>   wrist.

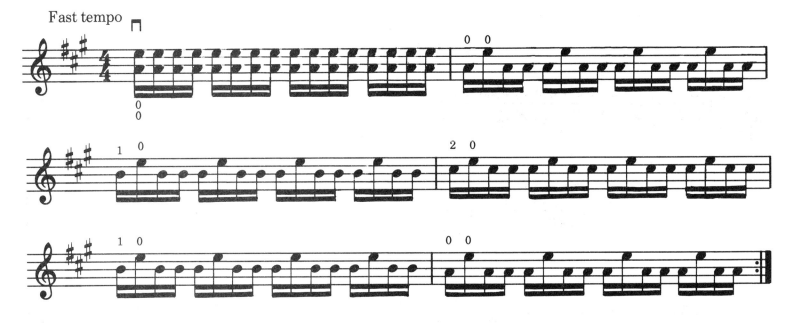

Practice on all strings.

String crossing at a medium (not fast) tempo.

As you move across the strings change your **arm height accordingly.**

Whether slurring or drawing separate strokes the **arm motion is the same.**

Fast string crossings are accomplished more with the wrist.
Slow string crossings are accomplished more with the arm.

Play "Soldier's Joy" at slow to medium speed.

Soldier's Joy

Lesson 20: The Low 2nd Finger

Place the 2nd finger very close to the 1st finger.
We will practice the new placement of the 2nd finger as we did previous left hand exercises.
1. Guitar position.
Slide the left hand smoothly back and forth along the fingerboard.
2. Come to rest in position (this is called first position).
3. Pluck the following pattern. The 1st finger and the 2nd finger are one-half step apart, and the 2nd and 3rd fingers are one whole step apart.
In other words, the 1st and 3rd fingers remain in their usual positions, the 2nd finger is closer to the 1st.

Practice on each string.

4. Violin in playing position: *Pizzicato.*
5. *Arco*

Keep your fingers down.

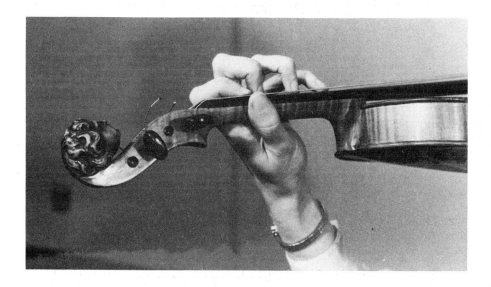

Figure 56

78

Upper half of the bow

Middle of the bow — short strokes

Divide your bow well.

Middle of the bow

G major scale – two octaves.

Upper half of bow
Arm high on G string, low on E string.

G major arpeggio

Put your 1st finger down with your 2nd.
Put your 2nd finger down with your 3rd.

Preparation for "She'll be Coming Round The Mountain"

Put your 2nd and 3rd fingers down with the 4th

She'll Be Coming Round The Mountain

Notice bow division markings.
Start this piece closer to the frog (lower half of the bow) than your are used to so you don't run out of bow on the dotted half-notes.

This piece also alternates between the low 2nd finger placement (C natural) and the high 2nd finger placement (F♯).

Skip To My Lou

middle to upper half

Lesson 21:

Practice this lesson and all following lessons for one week each.
Deep rich sound on the G string. Divide your bow well.

Will the Circle Be Unbroken

Hold your 3rd finger down where indicated by line. Arc the hand a little, if necessary, to keep the A string clear.

Figure 57
Arc the hand if necessary.

Cindy

arc the hand

Preparation for "Irish Washerwoman"

Start down-bow if you are playing all separate strokes. Start up-bow if slurring.
The slurs are optional.

Irish Washerwoman

More On Bow Division

Dividing the bow accurately and with foresight is very important so you don't run out of bow or leave too much bow at the end of a stroke. Your sound will be more consistent, controlled and refined if you are aware of your bow lengths.

When practicing the following exercise use a half bow for the quarter notes and a whole bow for the half notes.

LH – Lower Half – from the frog to the weight-middle of the bow.

UH – Upper Half – from the tip to weight-middle of the bow.

WB – Whole Bow.

Accurate Bow Division

WB UH   WB LH   WB UH   WB LH   WB UH

WB LH   WB UH   WB LH   WB UH   WB LH

WB UH   WB LH   WB UH   WB LH   WB

He's Got The Whole World In His Hand

Move the 3rd finger straight across the string from the note D to the note A. Don't lift it off the string.

Note the bow division markings:

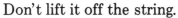

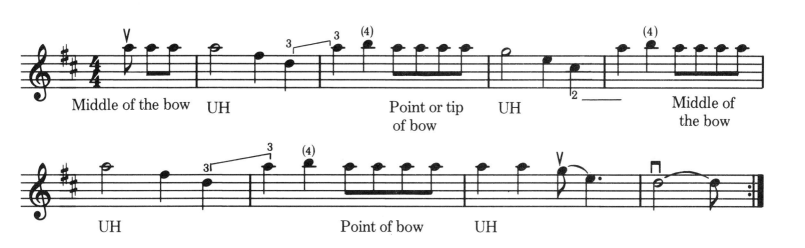

Middle of the bow   UH   Point or tip of bow   UH   Middle of the bow

UH   Point of bow   UH

83

Lesson 22: More on Bow Speed

Use the same amount of bow for all notes in this exercise.
Vary the speed of the stroke.

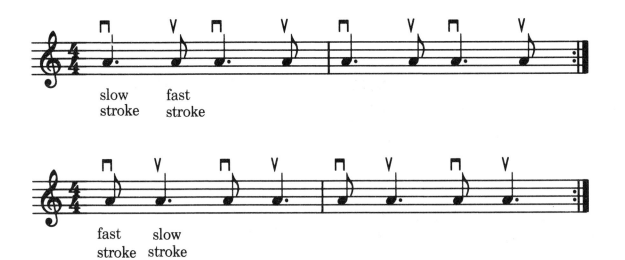

slow   fast
stroke stroke

fast   slow
stroke stroke

Oh, Them Golden Slippers

Lift off string

Basic Chords in C major

In the key of C major there are three basic chords with which to harmonize a tune:

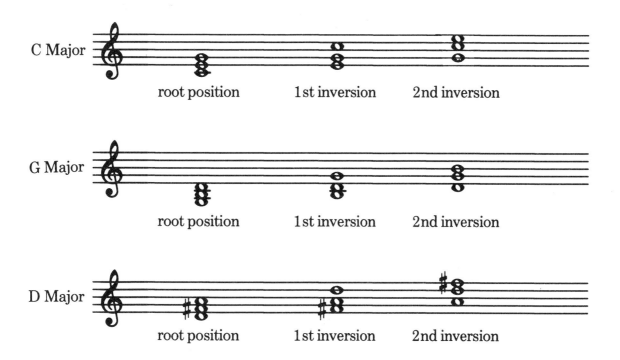

Hooked Bowing
Hooked bowing means: notes in the same bow stroke which are not played smoothly as in a slur, but have distinct articulation.

Let your arm drop a little after each small up-bow.
Articulate each up-bow note clearly.
Make each staccato sound crisp.

An example of hooked bowing.

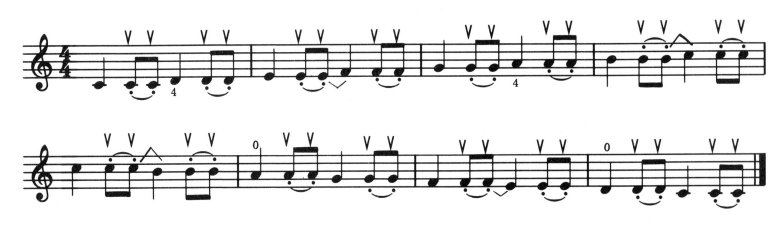

Turn back and play the melody to "Red River Valley."

Review "Irish Washerwoman," "Cindy," and "He's Got The Whole World In His Hand."

Lesson 23: The Left Hand (0 - 1 - 2 - 3 - 4)

Preparation for "Wabash Cannonball."

Wabash Cannonball

Gary Owen

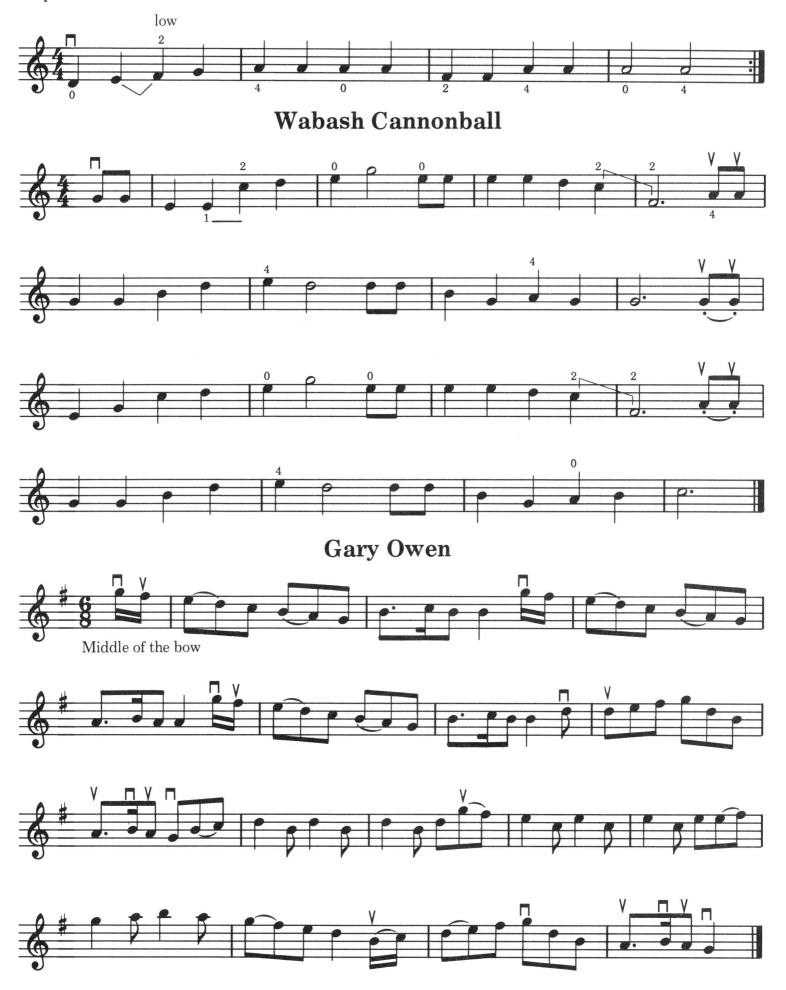

Lesson 24:

Double-stops, Hooked Bowing and Slurs

Preparation for "Cupid's Waltz" accompaniment. Smooth string crossings.
Move the bow along and use nearly a whole bow. Also practice with separate bow strokes – no slurs.

Note the hooked bowing and the combination of hooked bowing and slur.

Cupid's Waltz

Preparation for "Davy-Davy Nick-Nack"

Davy-Davy Nick-Nack

Upper half of bow

Lesson 25:

The Russki Reel

Upper half of the bow

Fine

Bowing practice
1. Upper Half of bow
2. Whole bow

Practice on all strings (G-D) (A-E)

Circle Strokes

Take your time

Believe Me If All Those Endearing Young Charms

Whenever the 3rd finger is indicated, put your 2nd and 3rd fingers down at the same time.
The 2nd finger should be placed in position to play the C natural (low 2nd finger).

Upper half of bow

Lesson 26:

Preparation for "Staten Island"

Staten Island

Faster String Crossings

Preparation for "Harvest Home" – A rather fast string crossing.
   Middle of the bow. Use little bow.
   Bow arm height at double-stop level.
   Use a wrist crossing primarily.
   Shoulder relaxed; passive.
   Let the weight of the bow sink in the string.

Harvest Home

Lesson 27: Whole Bow Strokes

A La Mode

Cincinnati

Turkey In The Straw

Play the staccato notes (𝅘𝅥) short

Middle of the bow

Stay on string

Use more bow here